Table of Content

Introduction.. 1
Chapter 1: Introduction to Wedding Planning....4
Chapter 2: Assessing Your Skills and Qualifications.. 8
Chapter 3: Understanding Your Target Market.12
Chapter 5: Legal and Regulatory Considerations.. 22
Chapter 6: Setting Up Your Business Operations.. 28
Chapter 7: Building Your Brand and Online Presence.. 35
Chapter 8: Acquiring Clients and Networking. 41
Chapter 9: Providing Exceptional Client Service. 46
Chapter 10: Growing Your Wedding Planning Business.. 50

Introduction

Welcome to "The Ultimate Guide on How To Start a Wedding Planning Business." If you have a passion for weddings, event planning, or entrepreneurship, this book is crafted just for you. It's designed to be your comprehensive roadmap, guiding you step-by-step towards launching your own successful wedding planning business.

Planning a wedding is no small feat. It's a specialized and intricate task that demands a keen eye for detail, impeccable organizational skills, boundless creativity, and top-notch communication abilities. As a wedding planner, you get the unique and joyous opportunity to be a part of one of the most significant moments in a couple's life, transforming their dream wedding into a beautiful reality.

Throughout this book, we'll dive deep into the many facets of starting and growing your wedding planning business. We'll begin with the foundational knowledge and essential skills you'll need for success. You'll learn how to define your target market, ensuring your services reach the right couples. We'll guide you through developing a solid business plan, a critical step for any budding entrepreneur. Additionally, we'll explore the legal and regulatory considerations crucial for smooth business operations.

In today's digital age, building a strong brand and online presence is more important than ever. We'll provide you with practical steps to establish your identity and reputation in the wedding industry. Attracting clients and networking effectively are key to your business's growth, and we'll share strategies to help you draw in potential clients and build valuable industry connections.

Exceptional client service is the cornerstone of any successful business, and for a wedding planner, it's even more vital. We'll explore ways to exceed your clients' expectations, manage vendor relationships seamlessly, and handle any challenges that may arise during the planning process.

Finally, we'll guide you on the journey of growing your wedding planning business. You'll learn tips on expanding your services, managing a team, and staying adaptable to industry trends to maintain a competitive edge.

Starting a wedding planning business requires dedication, hard work, and a passion for creating unforgettable experiences. Whether you're a seasoned event professional or just starting out in the industry, this book will equip you with the knowledge and tools you need to launch and thrive in your wedding planning venture.

So, let's dive in and embark on this exciting journey together!

Chapter 1: Introduction to Wedding Planning

Welcome to the exhilarating world of wedding planning! This chapter serves as your gateway into the field, offering a comprehensive introduction to what wedding planning entails. Whether you're a novice just dipping your toes in or someone with a bit of experience looking to refine your skills, this chapter will set the stage for your journey.

What is Wedding Planning?

Wedding planning is a beautiful blend of art and science. It involves meticulously organizing and coordinating every detail of a couple's wedding day to ensure it flows seamlessly and leaves a lasting impression. As a wedding planner, you'll wear many hats. Your responsibilities will range from helping couples choose the perfect venue and selecting reliable vendors to crafting detailed timelines and managing budgets. Your role is to bring the couple's vision to life while ensuring that every aspect of the day is executed flawlessly.

The Role of a Wedding Planner

Being a wedding planner is so much more than just coordinating events. You'll become a trusted advisor, a creative mastermind, and a soothing presence for your clients. Your guidance will be invaluable as you lead couples through the entire wedding planning process. You'll provide expert advice, brainstorm creative ideas, and keep everything impeccably organized. Your goal is to make the planning experience as enjoyable and stress-free as possible for the couple, culminating in a day that exceeds their expectations.

The Benefits of Starting a Wedding Planning Business

Starting your own wedding planning business comes with numerous perks. First and foremost, it allows you to turn your passion for weddings into a lucrative career. Imagine doing what you love and getting paid for it! Additionally, this career offers flexibility. You can choose to work on various events throughout the year, allowing you to maintain a work-life balance. Finally, you'll have the privilege of being part of one of the happiest days in a couple's life. Your efforts will leave a lasting impact, creating memories that they will cherish forever.

Skills and Traits for Success in Wedding Planning

While anyone can start a wedding planning business, certain skills and traits are essential for achieving success in this field. Let's delve into these key attributes:

1. **Organization:** Exceptional organizational skills are crucial. You'll need to keep track of countless details and deadlines, ensuring nothing slips through the cracks.
2. **Communication:** Strong communication skills are vital. You'll be dealing with clients, vendors, and various stakeholders, and clear, effective communication will ensure everyone is on the same page.
3. **Creativity:** Being able to think outside the box and come up with unique, personalized wedding ideas is a significant asset. Your creativity will set you apart and delight your clients.
4. **Flexibility:** Weddings often involve last-minute changes. Your ability to adapt and handle unexpected situations with grace will be invaluable.
5. **Attention to Detail:** From the layout of a reception room to the color of the flowers, every detail matters. A keen

eye for detail will ensure you create an unforgettable experience.

Conclusion

In this chapter, we've provided an overview of wedding planning and introduced you to the multifaceted role of a wedding planner. We've also discussed the benefits of starting your own wedding planning business and highlighted the essential skills and traits for success. As you continue reading this guide, you'll gain a deeper understanding of the wedding planning industry and learn how to build and grow a successful wedding planning business. So, let's dive in and explore the exciting world of wedding planning in more detail!

Chapter 2: Assessing Your Skills and Qualifications

Hey there! So, you're thinking about diving into the world of wedding planning, huh? That's fantastic! But before you get too far ahead of yourself, it's crucial to take a good, hard look at your skills and qualifications. After all, coordinating someone's wedding day means juggling a ton of different tasks and making sure everything goes off without a hitch. Let's break down what you need to succeed.

Evaluating Your Organizational Skills

First up, let's talk about organization. Picture this: a wedding involves coordinating timelines, managing vendor contracts, and keeping track of countless little details. It's like orchestrating a beautiful symphony where every note has to be spot on. Do you naturally excel at keeping things organized and juggling multiple tasks? Think back to times when you've had to plan events or manage projects. Did you handle it all seamlessly, or did you feel overwhelmed? Your past experiences can offer great insight here. If you've always been that person with color-coded spreadsheets and a knack for planning, you're on the right track.

Assessing Your Communication Skills

Next, let's chat about communication. As a wedding planner, you'll be the bridge between couples, vendors, and other stakeholders. Clear and effective communication is key to making sure everyone's on the same page. How good are you at expressing your ideas and instructions? Can you listen actively and really understand what your clients want? Maybe you've had a job where you had to negotiate or mediate between different parties. Reflect on those experiences. Strong communication skills aren't just about talking; they're about listening, understanding, and conveying information clearly.

Determining Your Creativity

Now, onto creativity. Weddings are personal and unique, and your clients will look to you to bring their vision to life. Do you have a flair for coming up with innovative ideas? Can you think outside the box and create themes and designs that are both cohesive and visually stunning? Consider your creative strengths. Maybe you're great at blending different elements to create a beautiful atmosphere, or you have a knack for turning a simple idea into a grand experience. Your ability to be creative will set you apart and help you deliver truly memorable weddings.

Evaluating Your Flexibility

Flexibility is another biggie. Weddings can be unpredictable – think sudden weather changes, last-minute cancellations, or unexpected hiccups. Can you roll with the punches and adapt on the fly? Reflect on situations where you had to think quickly and make adjustments. Were you able to stay calm and find solutions under pressure? Being flexible means having the resilience and resourcefulness to handle whatever comes your way, ensuring the day remains perfect despite any challenges.

Reviewing Your Attention to Detail

Lastly, let's focus on attention to detail. This might be the most critical skill of all. From seating charts to floral arrangements, every tiny element matters. Do you have an eagle eye for details? Are you meticulous in your planning and execution, ensuring nothing is overlooked? Think about times when you've had to pay close attention to details. Maybe you've caught small mistakes before they became big problems, or you've been praised for your thoroughness. Your knack for noticing and addressing even the smallest details can make or break a wedding day.

In summary, assessing your skills and qualifications is a vital step before you launch your wedding planning business. By evaluating your organizational skills, communication abilities, creativity, flexibility, and attention to detail, you'll get a clear picture of your strengths and areas for improvement. Understanding your capabilities will help you hone your skills and provide exceptional service to your clients. So take some time to reflect, and get ready to shine in the world of wedding planning!

Chapter 3: Understanding Your Target Market

Starting a wedding planning business is an exciting venture, but one of the first crucial steps you need to take is understanding your target market. This step is vital because by identifying and truly understanding your ideal clients, you can tailor your services to meet their specific needs and preferences. Moreover, this knowledge will help you effectively market your business to attract these clients. In this chapter, we'll explore why understanding your target market is so important and provide practical steps on how to identify and research your ideal clients.

The Importance of Understanding Your Target Market

Before you can successfully market your wedding planning business, it's essential to have a clear picture of who your target market is. Your target market is the specific group of people most likely to be interested in your services and who can benefit the most from what you offer. Grasping this concept helps you in several ways:

1. Tailoring Your Services

Knowing who your ideal clients are allows you to customize your services to meet their specific needs and preferences. For instance, if you primarily work with budget-conscious couples, you might offer more affordable packages or provide guidance on cost-saving options. Conversely, if your target market consists of luxury-seeking couples, you can focus on creating extravagant and high-end wedding experiences that cater to their desires.

2. Developing Effective Marketing Strategies

With a clear understanding of your target market, you can create targeted marketing campaigns that resonate with your ideal clients. By comprehending their values, interests, and pain points, you can craft messages and imagery that speak directly to their needs and desires. This increases the chances of attracting qualified leads and converting them into paying clients.

3. Identifying Opportunities for Growth

Understanding your target market can also help you identify untapped opportunities and new market segments to explore. By analyzing market trends and consumer behavior, you can uncover emerging needs or preferences that can serve as a basis for expanding your services or targeting a niche market.

Identifying Your Ideal Clients

To effectively understand your target market, you need to pinpoint your ideal clients. These are the individuals or couples who align perfectly with your business and are most likely to hire your services. Here are some steps to help you identify your ideal clients:

1. Evaluate Your Niche

Consider the specific niche within the wedding planning industry that you want to focus on. Are you drawn to destination weddings, cultural or religious weddings, eco-friendly weddings, or another specific type of celebration? By identifying your niche, you can narrow down your target market and tailor your services accordingly.

2. Conduct Market Research

Researching the wedding industry and your local market is essential in understanding your target market. Study industry trends, demographics, preferences, and your competition. Look for any underserved or unexplored segments where you can position your business and offer unique value.

3. Create Buyer Personas

To gain a deeper understanding of your ideal clients, create buyer personas. A buyer persona is a fictional representation of your target customer based on research and data. It includes demographic information, interests, motivations, challenges, and preferred wedding styles. This persona helps you put yourself in your clients' shoes and tailor your services to meet their specific needs.

4. Refine and Adjust

Understanding your target market is an ongoing process. As your business evolves and as you gain more experience, don't be afraid to refine and adjust your target market. Continuously gather feedback from your clients and monitor industry trends to ensure your services remain relevant and appealing.

By understanding your target market and catering to their needs, you can position your wedding planning business for success. Once you have a clear grasp of your ideal clients, you can start developing compelling marketing strategies, honing your services, and providing exceptional customer experiences. This understanding will be invaluable as you continue to build your business and grow in the wedding planning industry.

(Note: The information provided in this chapter is general in nature. It is recommended to conduct thorough market research and consult with industry professionals for a more comprehensive understanding of your target market.)

Chapter 4: Developing Your Business Plan

Creating a comprehensive business plan is essential for any entrepreneur looking to start a wedding planning business. Think of it as your roadmap, guiding you through the various stages of your venture, outlining your goals, strategies, and financial projections. A well-crafted business plan not only helps you stay on course but also plays a crucial role in securing funding and attracting potential clients. In this chapter, we'll delve into the key components of a wedding planning business plan and walk you through the process of developing one.

The Importance of a Business Plan

Before diving into the wedding planning industry, it's crucial to have a solid business plan. Imagine it as the blueprint of your business operations. It allows you to outline your objectives, identify your target market, set up a pricing structure, develop marketing strategies, and forecast financials. Having this clear direction helps you stay focused on your goals and keeps your business on track.

Moreover, a well-developed business plan is instrumental in attracting investors or securing financing. Banks and investors typically review business plans to assess the feasibility and profitability of a new venture. By showcasing your understanding of the industry, your target market, and your financial projections, you significantly increase your chances of obtaining the necessary funding for your wedding planning business.

Key Components of a Business Plan

1. **Executive Summary:** This section provides a snapshot of your wedding planning business, summarizing the key points of your business plan. Include information about your business concept, target market, competitive advantage, and financial projections. Think of it as your elevator pitch—brief but compelling.
2. **Company Description:** Here, you'll delve into the details of your wedding planning business. Include your company's legal structure, location, mission statement, and the services you plan to offer. Describe your unique selling proposition (USP) and how you aim to stand out from the competition.
3. **Market Analysis:** Conduct thorough research on the wedding planning

industry and your target market. Identify your ideal clients, their needs, and preferences. Analyze market trends, competition, and potential growth opportunities. Use this information to develop effective marketing strategies tailored to your target audience.

4. **Organization and Management:** Outline the organizational structure of your wedding planning business. Identify key team members, their roles, and responsibilities. Highlight any industry experience or certifications that you or your team members possess. This section showcases the strength and expertise of your team.

5. **Services and Pricing:** Detail the range of services you plan to offer and determine your pricing structure. Consider factors such as time, resources, and market demand when setting your prices. Clearly explain the value and benefits your services will provide to clients. Transparency here builds trust with potential clients.

6. **Marketing and Sales Strategies:** Outline your marketing and sales approaches to attract and retain clients. Consider both traditional and digital marketing tactics, such as advertising, social media, networking events, and partnerships with vendors. Identify your

competitive advantage and emphasize it in your marketing materials.
7. **Financial Projections:** Develop a financial forecast for your wedding planning business, including projected revenue, expenses, and profitability. Consider factors such as start-up costs, ongoing expenses, pricing, and market demand. Create a realistic timeline for reaching profitability and outline your funding needs, if applicable.
8. **Implementation Plan:** Lay out the steps you will take to launch and grow your wedding planning business. Develop a timeline for completing key tasks, such as obtaining necessary licenses and permits, building a client base, and expanding your services. Set measurable goals and milestones to track your progress.

Refining Your Business Plan

Once you've drafted your business plan, it's essential to review and refine it periodically. As you gain more insights and experience in the wedding planning industry, you may need to adjust your strategies to stay competitive. Regularly reassess your financial projections, target market, and marketing tactics to ensure they align with your business goals.
Remember, a business plan is a dynamic document that should evolve as your business

grows. Continuously monitor and update your plan to reflect changes in the industry, market trends, and client preferences.

Conclusion

Developing a comprehensive business plan is a crucial step in starting a wedding planning business. It provides a roadmap for your operations, helps secure funding, attracts potential clients, and keeps you focused on your goals. By incorporating the key components discussed in this chapter, you can create a strong foundation for your wedding planning business and increase your chances of success. So, take the time to craft a detailed and thoughtful business plan—it's an investment that will pay off in the long run.

Chapter 5: Legal and Regulatory Considerations

Starting your wedding planning business is an exciting venture, but it's important to be aware of the legal and regulatory considerations that come with it. Ensuring you comply with these guidelines not only protects your business but also helps you build a reliable and reputable service for your clients. Let's dive into the key legal and regulatory aspects you need to consider.

Licensing and Permits

One of the first steps in setting up your wedding planning business is to research and obtain the necessary licenses and permits required by your local and state authorities. These requirements can vary widely depending on your location, so it's crucial to contact the appropriate agencies to determine what you need to operate legally. Here are some common licenses and permits you might need:

1. **Business License:** This is a general requirement for operating any type of business. It ensures you comply with local regulations and is often the first step in legitimizing your business.

2. **Vendor Permits:** If you plan to collaborate with venues, caterers, or other vendors, they might require you to have specific permits to work with them legally.
3. **Sales Tax Permit:** Depending on your location, you might need to collect and remit sales tax on your services. Research the sales tax regulations in your area to stay compliant.

Thoroughly researching these requirements will help you avoid legal issues down the line. Contact your local small business administration or chamber of commerce for guidance on the specific requirements in your area.

Contracts and Liability

Contracts are a cornerstone of running a wedding planning business. They protect both you and your clients by clearly outlining expectations and responsibilities. Before you provide any services, it's essential to have a well-drafted and legally binding contract in place. When creating your contract, consider including these elements:

1. **Services Provided:** Clearly outline the services you will offer, including the

scope of work and specific tasks you will handle.
2. **Payment Terms:** Specify your payment structure, including deposits, installment plans, and final payment deadlines.
3. **Cancellation and Refund Policies:** State your policies regarding cancellations, rescheduling, and refunds.
4. **Liability and Insurance:** Consult with an attorney to ensure you have appropriate liability insurance to protect your business in case of accidents or damages.
5. **Intellectual Property Rights:** Clarify ownership and usage rights of any intellectual property, such as designs or concepts, created during the planning process.

Seeking legal counsel while drafting your contracts is highly recommended to ensure they are comprehensive and enforceable.

Data Protection and Privacy

As a wedding planner, you'll handle sensitive and personal information about your clients, including their contact details, budgets, and preferences. Prioritizing data protection and privacy is essential to maintain your clients' trust. Consider implementing the following measures:

1. **Secure Storage:** Ensure that physical or digital files containing client information are stored securely and accessible only to authorized personnel.
2. **Confidentiality Agreements:** Have clients sign confidentiality agreements, especially if you'll be sharing their information with vendors or subcontractors.
3. **Data Encryption:** Use encryption software to protect electronic files and communication channels.
4. **Compliance with Data Protection Laws:** Familiarize yourself with the data protection laws in your jurisdiction, such as the GDPR in the European Union or the CCPA in the United States.

Always inform your clients about how their personal information will be used and obtain their consent to process and store their data.

Insurance Coverage

Insurance is an essential aspect of protecting your wedding planning business from unexpected events and liabilities. Although it might seem like an extra expense, having the appropriate insurance coverage can safeguard your business and provide peace of mind. Consider the following types of insurance for your wedding planning business:

1. **General Liability Insurance:** Protects you from claims of bodily injury, property damage, or personal injury that might occur during the planning or execution of a wedding.
2. **Professional Liability Insurance:** Also known as errors and omissions insurance, this coverage protects you from claims of negligence or mistakes in your professional services.
3. **Property Insurance:** Covers damages to your office space, equipment, or inventory.
4. **Cyber Liability Insurance:** Protects against cyber threats, including data breaches, identity theft, and computer damage caused by cyberattacks.

Consult with an insurance agent specializing in small businesses to determine the appropriate coverage for your wedding planning business.

Conclusion

Understanding the legal and regulatory considerations of starting a wedding planning business is crucial for a successful and compliant operation. By obtaining the necessary licenses, having solid contracts, prioritizing data protection, and securing appropriate insurance coverage, you can ensure the longevity and growth of your wedding planning venture. Remember to consult with legal and financial professionals to tailor your legal approach to your specific business needs.

By taking these steps, you'll be well on your way to building a reputable and successful wedding planning business that your clients can trust. Happy planning!

Chapter 6: Setting Up Your Business Operations

Setting up your business operations is a crucial step in launching your wedding planning business. It involves establishing the necessary systems, processes, and resources to efficiently run your business and deliver exceptional services to your clients. In this chapter, we'll explore the key aspects of setting up your business operations and provide you with practical tips to ensure a smooth and successful start.

Determine Your Business Structure

One of the first steps in setting up your business operations is determining the legal structure of your wedding planning business. The most common options include a sole proprietorship, partnership, limited liability company (LLC), or corporation. Each structure has its own advantages and disadvantages, so it's important to carefully consider which option aligns with your goals, risk tolerance, and long-term plans.

A sole proprietorship is the simplest form and easiest to set up, but it doesn't offer personal liability protection. A partnership involves two or more people sharing the business responsibilities and profits. An LLC provides personal liability protection without the complexity of a corporation, making it a popular choice for many small business owners. Lastly, a corporation offers the most protection but involves more regulatory requirements and can be more expensive to set up.

Choose a Business Name

Selecting a memorable and meaningful name for your wedding planning business is an important part of establishing your brand identity. Consider a name that reflects your unique style, values, and target market. It should be easy to pronounce, spell, and remember. Before finalizing your business name, conduct a thorough search to ensure that it is not already in use and register it with the appropriate authorities.

Your business name is often the first impression potential clients will have, so make it count. Think about what makes your business special and how you want to be perceived in the industry. A catchy, relevant name can help you stand out and attract your ideal clients.

Secure Necessary Business Licenses and Permits

Before you can legally operate your wedding planning business, it's essential to obtain the necessary licenses and permits. The specific requirements vary depending on your location, so research the local regulations and reach out to the relevant governing bodies to ensure compliance. Some common licenses and permits you may need include a business license, vendor permits, and a sales tax permit.

Failing to secure the proper licenses can result in fines and disrupt your business operations. It's better to handle these administrative tasks upfront so you can focus on serving your clients without legal worries.

Establish Your Office Space

Creating a conducive and professional office space is vital for the smooth operation of your business. Decide whether you will work from a home office or lease a commercial space. Regardless of your choice, ensure that your workspace is well-organized, comfortable, and equipped with essential tools such as a computer, phone system, printer, and office supplies. Don't forget to set up a dedicated area for client meetings and consultations.

A well-designed office space can boost your productivity and create a positive impression on clients. If you choose a home office, make sure it's separate from your personal living space to maintain a professional atmosphere.

Implement Efficient Systems and Processes

Efficient systems and processes are the backbone of any successful wedding planning business. Streamline your operations by implementing tools and technologies that help you manage client communication, project timelines, budgeting, and vendor coordination. Consider investing in project management software, customer relationship management (CRM) tools, and accounting software to automate repetitive tasks and enhance productivity.

Automation can save you time and reduce errors, allowing you to focus more on your clients and creative aspects of planning weddings. The right tools will help you stay organized and keep everything running smoothly.

Build a Reliable Vendor Network

As a wedding planner, having a reliable network of vendors is crucial to deliver exceptional services to your clients. Start building relationships with wedding venues, caterers, florists, photographers, and other industry professionals. Attend industry events, participate in networking groups, and collaborate with vendors on styled shoots or wedding showcases. Establishing trust and strong partnerships will not only enhance the quality of your services but also expand your referral network.

A strong vendor network can make or break your business. When you have trusted partners, you can ensure that every aspect of the wedding day goes off without a hitch.

Set Up Financial Systems

Managing your finances effectively is essential for the long-term success of your wedding planning business. Set up a separate business bank account to keep your personal and business finances separate. Implement a bookkeeping system to track income, expenses, and cash flow. Consider hiring an accountant or using accounting software to ensure accurate and compliant financial records.

Good financial management is the foundation of a sustainable business. Keeping your finances in order will help you make informed decisions and stay on top of your obligations.

Create Contracts and Policies

To protect your business and provide clarity to your clients, create comprehensive contracts and policies. Your contracts should outline the scope of services, payment terms, cancellation policies, liability, and intellectual property rights. It's important to consult with a legal professional to ensure that your contracts are legally binding and comply with industry standards and regulations.

Clear contracts can prevent misunderstandings and protect you from potential legal issues. They set the expectations for both you and your clients, ensuring a smooth working relationship.

Develop a Disaster Preparedness Plan

In the event of unforeseen circumstances or emergencies, having a disaster preparedness plan in place is essential. Identify potential risks and develop strategies to mitigate them. This may include having backup vendors, contingency plans for outdoor weddings, and protocols for handling crises. By being proactive and prepared, you can minimize disruptions and ensure a seamless experience for your clients.

A well-thought-out disaster plan will give you and your clients peace of mind. It shows that you're prepared for any situation, which builds trust and confidence.

Conclusion

Setting up your business operations is a critical step towards establishing a successful wedding planning business. By thoughtfully determining your business structure, securing necessary licenses, establishing efficient systems, building strong vendor relationships, and implementing financial and disaster preparedness plans, you can position your business for growth and success. Remember, attention to detail and a commitment to exceptional service will set you apart in the competitive wedding planning industry.

As you embark on this journey, take the time to lay a strong foundation. Each decision you make in the setup phase will have long-lasting effects on your business's success. Stay focused, be diligent, and always strive to exceed your clients' expectations. With these preparations, you'll be well on your way to creating unforgettable wedding experiences and building a thriving business.

Chapter 7: Building Your Brand and Online Presence

Building a strong brand and establishing a compelling online presence are essential steps for success in the wedding planning industry. Your brand sets you apart from your competitors and leaves a lasting impression on potential clients. In this chapter, we'll explore strategies to build your brand and create a strong online presence that attracts your target market.

Understanding Your Brand Identity

Before you start building your brand, it's crucial to have a clear understanding of your brand identity. Think of your brand identity as the essence of who you are as a wedding planner. It encompasses the values, personality, and image you want to convey to your clients. It represents what you stand for and what makes you unique.

To get started, reflect on these questions:

- What is your unique selling point? What sets you apart from other wedding planners?
- What are your core values and beliefs? How are they reflected in your business?
- What is the overall tone and personality of your brand? Is it elegant and sophisticated, or fun and quirky?
- What emotions do you want your brand to evoke in your clients?
- How do you want to be perceived by your target market?

By answering these questions, you'll have a solid foundation to build your brand upon. Your brand identity will guide all your branding efforts and ensure consistency across all touchpoints.

Creating a Memorable Logo and Visual Identity

One of the most important elements of your brand is your logo and visual identity. Your logo will be the symbol that represents your business and will be displayed on your website, social media profiles, business cards, and marketing materials. It should be unique, memorable, and visually appealing.

When creating your logo, consider hiring a professional graphic designer who specializes in branding. They'll take into account your brand identity, target market, and industry trends to design a logo that resonates with your audience. Your logo should reflect your brand's personality and evoke the emotions you want your clients to feel when they see it.

In addition to your logo, develop a consistent visual identity for your brand. This includes choosing a color palette, typography, and visual elements that align with your brand identity. Consistency across all your marketing materials will help create a cohesive and recognizable brand.

Building an Engaging Website

In today's digital age, having a professional website is crucial for any business, including wedding planning. Your website serves as a virtual storefront where potential clients can learn more about your services, view your portfolio, and contact you. Here are some tips for building an engaging website:

- Choose a clean and user-friendly design that showcases your brand and is easy to navigate.

- Use high-quality images that highlight your work and talent.
- Clearly state your services and pricing.
- Include testimonials from satisfied clients to build trust and credibility.
- Optimize your website for search engines to increase your online visibility.
- Make sure your website is mobile-friendly to cater to the growing number of users browsing on smartphones and tablets.

Your website should be a reflection of your brand, providing a seamless and enjoyable experience for visitors.

Harnessing the Power of Social Media

Social media platforms are valuable tools for building your brand and connecting with your target market. Each platform has its unique advantages, so it's important to understand your ideal clients and choose the platforms where they are most active. Here are some tips for effectively using social media:

- Create engaging and shareable content that showcases your expertise and provides value to your audience.
- Use high-quality images and videos to grab attention and tell your brand story.

- Engage with your audience by responding to comments, messages, and reviews.
- Collaborate with influencers or other wedding professionals to expand your reach.
- Stay consistent with your brand identity across all social media channels.
- Utilize targeted ads to reach a larger audience and promote your services.

Social media is a powerful tool for building relationships with potential clients and showcasing your work in a dynamic and interactive way.

Online Reviews and Testimonials

Positive reviews and testimonials have a significant impact on potential clients' decision-making process. They provide social proof and build trust in your brand. Encourage your satisfied clients to leave reviews on platforms such as Google, Yelp, and WeddingWire.

When requesting testimonials, guide your clients by providing specific questions to answer or asking them to share their favorite part of working with you. This will help them provide more detailed and compelling testimonials.

Monitoring and Adjusting Your Online Presence

Building your brand and online presence is an ongoing process. It's important to regularly monitor your online presence and make adjustments as needed. Stay up to date with industry trends and best practices to ensure that your brand remains relevant and appealing to your target market.

Monitor your social media platforms, website analytics, and online reviews to gain insights into your audience's preferences and engagement. Use this data to refine your strategies and make informed decisions moving forward.

Remember, building a strong brand and online presence takes time and effort. Stay consistent in your messaging, engage with your audience, and always strive to provide exceptional service. By doing so, you'll create a memorable brand that attracts your ideal clients and sets you apart from your competitors.

Chapter 8: Acquiring Clients and Networking

In the wedding planning industry, acquiring clients and building a robust network are vital for the success of your business. Think of this chapter as your go-to guide for expanding your client base and establishing meaningful connections within the industry.

Identifying Your Target Clients

Before you can effectively acquire clients, it's crucial to identify and understand your target market. Who are the people you want to serve? Are they young couples just starting out, or are they older, more established couples looking for something grander? Are they dreaming of a traditional wedding, or do they lean towards a modern and unconventional approach?

Understanding your target clients helps you tailor your services and marketing efforts to meet their specific needs and preferences. Conducting market research is key here. Create detailed buyer personas to gain insight into their desires, pain points, and motivations. This information will help you craft personalized marketing messages and offer services that resonate with your target market.

Developing an Effective Marketing Strategy

To acquire clients, you need a well-rounded marketing strategy that reaches and appeals to your target market. Here are some key strategies to consider:

1. **Create a Professional Website:** Your website is your online storefront. It should reflect your brand's personality and unique selling points. Include a portfolio of past weddings, a list of services offered, pricing information, testimonials, and a contact form for inquiries. Make it visually appealing and easy to navigate.
2. **Search Engine Optimization (SEO):** Optimize your website for search engines by using relevant keywords, creating quality content, and ensuring it's mobile-friendly. This will help potential clients find you when they search for wedding planners in your area.
3. **Social Media Presence:** Utilize platforms like Instagram, Facebook, and Pinterest to showcase your work, engage with your audience, and

establish credibility. Share visually appealing images and videos, collaborate with influencers, and encourage clients to tag and share their experiences.

4. **Wedding Directories and Bridal Magazines:** List your business in popular wedding directories and consider advertising in bridal magazines to reach a wider audience. These platforms are often frequented by couples actively seeking wedding planning services.
5. **Referrals and Testimonials:** Encourage satisfied clients to leave positive reviews and testimonials on your website, social media platforms, and other wedding planning review websites. Word-of-mouth referrals are powerful in the wedding industry, so make sure your clients are impressed with your services.
6. **Wedding Expos and Networking Events:** Participate in local wedding expos and attend industry networking events to connect with potential clients and build relationships with other professionals in the wedding industry. Consider having a visually appealing booth and offering promotional materials to leave a lasting impression.

Nurturing Relationships and Networking

Networking is essential for building a strong client base and establishing credibility within the wedding planning industry. Here are some tips to help you effectively network:

1. **Participate in Wedding Industry Associations:** Join local and national wedding industry associations to connect with other professionals, gain industry insights, and access networking events. These associations often provide opportunities for collaboration and referrals.
2. **Collaborate with Other Wedding Professionals:** Build relationships with photographers, florists, caterers, venues, and other professionals in the wedding industry. Offer your services as a preferred or recommended wedding planner to their clients in exchange for referrals.
3. **Attend Industry Events:** Attend trade shows, conferences, and workshops specifically tailored for wedding professionals. These events provide opportunities to learn from industry experts, meet potential clients, and stay updated on industry trends.

4. **Provide Exceptional Client Service:** Delight your clients with exceptional service and exceed their expectations. Happy clients are more likely to refer you to their friends and family, leading to a steady stream of new clients.
5. **Follow Up:** After working with a client, follow up with a handwritten thank-you note or a personalized email expressing your gratitude. This small gesture goes a long way in building lasting relationships and generating referrals.

Remember, acquiring clients and networking require patience and persistence. It takes time to establish your reputation and build a strong network within the industry. Stay proactive, continue refining your marketing strategies, and consistently deliver outstanding service to stand out in the competitive wedding planning market.

Chapter 9: Providing Exceptional Client Service

As a wedding planner, providing exceptional client service is crucial for your success and reputation in the industry. Your clients are entrusting you with one of the most important days of their lives, and it's your responsibility to ensure their experience is seamless, memorable, and stress-free. In this chapter, we'll dive into strategies and best practices for delivering exceptional client service in the wedding planning business.

Understanding the Client's Vision

To provide exceptional client service, it's essential to fully understand and embrace your client's vision for their wedding day. Start by taking the time to listen to their ideas, preferences, and expectations. Ask open-ended questions to gain a deeper understanding of their style, theme, and desired atmosphere. The more you know about their vision, the better equipped you'll be to meet their needs and exceed their expectations.

Tailoring Your Services

Every client is unique, and their needs can vary widely. To provide exceptional client service, it's important to tailor your services to meet their specific requirements. Offer flexible packages or customizable options that allow clients to choose the level of assistance they need. Some may only require guidance during the planning process, while others might want you to handle every detail from start to finish. By offering personalized services, you can ensure each client receives the attention and support they deserve.

Effective Communication

Clear and open communication is key to providing exceptional client service. Establish regular communication channels and be responsive to your client's inquiries, whether through email, phone calls, or meetings. Keep them updated on the progress of their wedding plans, provide timely reminders, and promptly address any concerns or issues that arise. Maintaining effective communication will build trust and confidence with your clients.

Going the Extra Mile

Exceptional client service means going above and beyond to exceed expectations. Surprise your clients with thoughtful gestures or personalized touches that show you genuinely care about their special day. It could be something as simple as sending a handwritten note or recommending a unique vendor that aligns with their vision. By going the extra mile, you'll create a memorable experience for your clients and leave a lasting impression.

Handling Challenges

In the wedding planning business, challenges are inevitable. How you handle these challenges sets you apart in terms of client service. Be proactive and transparent in communicating any potential issues and offer viable solutions. Take responsibility for any mistakes and work diligently to rectify them. By demonstrating professionalism and a willingness to resolve problems, you'll build trust and maintain strong client relationships.

Following Up

Providing exceptional client service doesn't end on the wedding day. Follow up with your clients after their special day to ensure their satisfaction and gather feedback. Send a thank-you note or email expressing your gratitude for their trust in you. Ask for their input on their overall experience and if there are any areas for improvement. Respond to their feedback and use it to enhance your services in the future.

Conclusion

Providing exceptional client service is the cornerstone of a successful wedding planning business. By understanding your client's vision, tailoring your services, maintaining effective communication, going the extra mile, handling challenges with professionalism, and following up, you'll exceed expectations and create lasting relationships with your clients. Your dedication to exceptional client service will not only lead to satisfied clients but also positive word-of-mouth referrals, which are invaluable in this industry.

Embrace these strategies, and you'll build a reputation for excellence that will set your wedding planning business apart from the competition.

Chapter 10: Growing Your Wedding Planning Business

Growing your wedding planning business is an exhilarating journey that promises long-term success and sustainability. It's about extending your reach, drawing in more clients, and boosting your revenue. In this chapter, we'll dive into various strategies and techniques to help you achieve growth in your wedding planning business.

1. Expanding Your Service Offerings

One fantastic way to grow your wedding planning business is by expanding your service offerings. By providing additional services, you can appeal to a broader range of clients and open up new revenue streams. Think about adding services like floral design, event styling, or destination wedding planning to meet the diverse needs of couples.

Before diving into new service offerings, it's crucial to thoroughly assess the market demand and ensure you have the skills and resources to deliver top-notch results. Conducting market research will help you pinpoint which services are in demand and align with your target market's preferences. Additionally, consider partnering with other wedding professionals who specialize in these new services. This can enhance your capabilities and credibility, making your business more attractive to potential clients.

2. Targeting New Market Segments

To grow your wedding planning business, exploring new market segments is essential. By diversifying your client base, you can extend your business's reach and uncover new opportunities. Start by conducting market research to identify potential market segments that align with your business goals and capabilities.

For example, you might look into catering to same-sex couples, destination weddings, or cultural weddings. Tailor your marketing messages and branding to resonate with these specific segments, showcasing your understanding and expertise in their unique wedding needs. This targeted approach can help you connect with a wider audience and grow your business.

3. Leveraging Online Marketing

In today's digital age, having a robust online presence is crucial for business growth. Utilize various online marketing strategies to boost your visibility, attract potential clients, and build your brand reputation.

Optimize your website with search engine optimization (SEO) techniques to improve your rankings in search engine results. Make sure your website is user-friendly, mobile-responsive, and showcases your portfolio, testimonials, and service offerings. Investing in professional photography and videography to display your past weddings can leave a lasting impression on visitors.

Engage in content marketing by regularly publishing informative blog posts, articles, or videos that provide value to your target audience. Share useful tips, trends, and inspiration related to wedding planning. This positions you as an industry expert and helps build trust with potential clients.

Harness the power of social media platforms like Instagram, Facebook, and Pinterest to showcase your work, engage with your audience, and attract new clients. Create visually appealing content, collaborate with influencers or other wedding vendors, and actively participate in relevant wedding-related communities and forums. This will help you maintain a strong online presence and reach a wider audience.

4. Building Relationships and Referrals

Building strong relationships with both clients and fellow wedding professionals is crucial for growing your wedding planning business. Word-of-mouth referrals can be a powerful marketing tool, so focus on delivering exceptional service to your current clients to encourage them to recommend you to others.

Seek opportunities to collaborate with other wedding vendors, such as photographers, caterers, or venue owners. By forming mutually beneficial partnerships, you can expand your network, gain access to new clients, and receive referrals. Attend industry networking events, join professional associations, and participate in trade shows or conferences to connect with other wedding professionals.

Additionally, consider implementing a referral program that incentivizes clients or fellow vendors to refer new clients to your business. Offer referral rewards or discounts to those who successfully bring in new business. This not only encourages referrals but also strengthens relationships with your existing network.

5. Continuous Learning and Professional Development

The wedding planning industry is constantly evolving, with new trends, technologies, and techniques emerging. To stay competitive and fuel the growth of your business, it is crucial to commit to continuous learning and professional development.

Stay updated on the latest industry trends and attend relevant workshops, conferences, and webinars. This allows you to expand your knowledge, learn new skills, and discover innovative ideas to enhance your service offerings. Additionally, consider investing in certifications or specialized training programs that further validate your expertise and set you apart from competitors.

By continuously learning and adapting to industry changes, you can position yourself as a knowledgeable and trusted wedding planner, attracting more clients and driving business growth.

Conclusion

Growing your wedding planning business involves strategic planning, innovation, and a commitment to excellence. By expanding your service offerings, targeting new market segments, leveraging online marketing, building relationships, and continuously investing in your professional development, you can successfully grow your business and achieve long-term success in the wedding planning industry.

www.ingramcontent.com/pod-product-compliance
Lightning Source LLC
Chambersburg PA
CBHW070134230526
45472CB00004B/1526